The Invisible War

A Guide To Understanding Body Dysmorphic Disorder

Breanna Parkes

Table of Contents

Introduction

A lot of people may be obsessed by their appearance, with a perceived flaw leading to immense distress and anxiety. Most of us reflect on how to improve our appearance from time to time, which is perfectly normal. This is how most of us function, because we all care about how we look to others. We all want to be the best versions of ourselves, hundred percent presentable all the time. With perfectly proportionate noses, 5 o'clock shadows in all the right places, and perfect bikini bodies, who wouldn't want to look like that? We're not here to judge, we understand.

But for some people, this focus on appearance can become extreme and intrusive, to the point where it dominates their lives.]When this reflection and preoccupation takes over your life to the point where it interferes with daily functioning, it may be indicative of a condition known as body dysmorphic disorder (BDD).

It is a mental health condition where a person becomes fixated on one or more perceived physical flaws. It is a condition that can have a profound impact on a person's quality of life and can lead to significant distress and impairment. What is more disturbing is that it may be under-recognized because people with BDD are often afraid or ashamed to seek help or their habits and obsessions are mistaken as a phase.

The impact of Body Dysmorphic Disorder on your life can be debilitating, especially if left untreated. Young people with this disorder can face significant challenges in their academic and social lives. The good news is that there are effective treatments available for BDD. With treatment, people with BDD can learn to manage their symptoms and live fulfilling lives.

This book is designed to provide information and support to those affected by BDD, as well as to their family and friends. We start of by explaining what body dysmorphic disorder is, the historical significance of this disease and how the definition has evolved over time.

The etiology, pathogenesis and risk factors will be discussed in the next few chapters. We will provide detailed information about the various symptoms associated with this disorder and how it presents in different genders across all age groups. The impact of BDD on quality of life will also be explored.

We then discuss screening and diagnosis of this disease along with core clinical features. The treatments available are then reviewed, before we provide a section discussing how to support someone with BDD.
By the end of this book, you will have a greater understanding of BDD and how to best support someone affected by this disorder.

We hope that through reading this book, you will develop a better understanding of this condition and feel equipped to support yourself or someone you know who is affected by BDD. If you are affected by BDD, we hope that this book will provide you with some useful information and help you on your journey to recovery. If you know someone with BDD, we hope that it will give you a better understanding of the condition and how you can support your loved one.

Please note that this book is not intended to replace professional medical advice. If you are concerned about your own health or the health of someone you know, please seek help from a qualified healthcare professional.

Chapter 1: What is Body Dysmorphic Disorder?

Body dysmorphic disorder (BDD) is a mental health condition where a person spends a lot of time worrying about and obsessing over their appearance. People with BDD often have a distorted view of how they look and see themselves as ugly or deformed, even when others don't see it. This can lead to a preoccupation with appearance and excessive grooming, mirror checking and reassurance seeking behaviors. BDD can have a profound effect on a person's life, impacting their work, school and social life.

This perceived defect can be all consuming and can lead to avoidance of social situations, isolation and even suicidal thoughts. It is important to realize that BDD is a real mental health condition that requires treatment. If you or someone you know is struggling with BDD, there is help available.

People with BDD often fixate on a particular area of their appearance that they perceive as defective. This can be anything from their skin, hair, nose, weight or any other physical feature. They will often spend a lot of time looking in the mirror, comparing themselves to others and engaging in excessive grooming behaviors. People with BDD may also frequently ask for reassurance from others about their appearance.

BDD can have a significant impact on a person's quality of life. It can interfere with work, school and social activities. People with BDD may miss work or school due to avoidance of social situations. They may also isolate themselves from friends and family. In severe cases, BDD can lead to suicidal thoughts and behaviors.

History of Body Dysmorphic Disorder

The first descriptions of body dysmorphic disorder date back to the late 1800s. In 1891, Enrico Morselli, an Italian psychiatrist, described a patient with "dysmorphophobia" who was preoccupied with the idea that he had a facial deformity. The term was derived from "dysmorphia" meaning deformity, and "phobia" meaning fear. He described the disease as "the sudden appearance and fixation in the consciousness of the idea of one's own deformity."
The next major historical reference to "dysmorphophobia" was by the French psychiatrist Pierre Janet in 1899. Janet described a patient with intense anxiety and avoidance behaviors related to her belief that she had a facial deformity.

Freud also made reference to body dysmorphic disorder in "Wolf Man"" case study. Freud described a patient who was fixated on the idea that he had a physical deformity, which caused him great distress.

In 1980, dysmorphophobia was included in the American Psychiatric Association's Diagnostic and Statistical Manual as an "atypical somatoform condition" with no diagnostic criteria. It wasn't until 1987 that the first formal diagnostic criteria for body dysmorphic disorder were proposed. These criteria were published in the Diagnostic and Statistical Manual of Mental Disorders (DSM III-R). The current DSM-5 criteria for BDD were published in 2013.

Prevalence of Body Dysmorphic Disorder

Body dysmorphic disorder is a relatively common mental health condition. The prevalence of BDD in the general population is estimated to be between 1-2%. In one study, the prevalence of BDD in college students was found to be 2.4%. Other studies have found that the prevalence of BDD in psychiatric patients is between 4-15%.

The prevalence of BDD varies across different studies due to methodological differences, such as the use of different populations and different assessment instruments. It is also likely that the prevalence of BDD is underestimated because people with the condition are often too ashamed to seek help. They may also not be aware that their preoccupation with their appearance is a sign of a mental health condition.

Under recognition of BDD is a significant problem because the condition can have a profound negative impact on a person's quality of life. BDD is associated with high levels of psychological distress and functional impairment. It is also associated with a high risk of suicide.

Classification of BDD

The classification of Body Dysmorphic Disorder has changed over time. In the DSM-III, BDD was classified as an "atypical somatoform condition". This means that it was recognized as a real mental health condition, but there were no formal diagnostic criteria. In the DSM-III-R, BDD was classified as a somatoform disorder. Somatoform disorders are mental health conditions where there are physical symptoms that cannot be explained by a medical condition.

In the DSM-5, BDD was reclassified as a body-image disorder. This is in recognition of the fact that BDD is primarily a preoccupation with appearance, rather than physical symptoms. It is now classified under the new category "obsessive–compulsive and related disorders", which includes other conditions such as obsessive-compulsive disorder and trichotillomania.

Chapter 2: How Do I Know If I Have It?

Body dysmorphic disorder is a mental health condition that is characterized by a preoccupation with one or more perceived defects or flaws in appearance. People with BDD often spend a lot of time thinking about their appearance, and may engage in repetitive behaviors such as mirror checking, skin picking, and reassurance seeking. BDD can cause significant distress and impairment in social, occupational, or other important areas of functioning.

The following are some of the core clinical features of BDD:

People with BDD are preoccupied with one or more perceived defects or flaws in their appearance. They may spend a lot of time thinking about their appearance and may compare themselves with others.

People with BDD may engage in repetitive behaviors such as mirror checking, skin picking, and reassurance seeking. These behaviors are often an attempt to relieve the anxiety and distress caused by the person's appearance concerns.

BDD can cause significant distress and impairment in social, occupational, or other important areas of functioning. People with BDD may avoid social situations, miss work or school, and have difficulty maintaining relationships.

The preoccupation with appearance must not be better explained by another mental health condition. For example, a person with an eating disorder may be concerned with their weight, but this would not be classified as BDD.

Diagnosing BDD

The diagnosis of BDD is made by a mental health professional such as a psychiatrist, psychologist, or clinical social worker. The mental health professional will ask questions about the person's symptoms and perform a psychological evaluation. The evaluation may include a physical exam to rule out any physical causes of the person's distress.

Diagnostic Criteria for Body Dysmorphic Disorder

The DSM-5 includes the following diagnostic criteria for BDD:

1. Preoccupation with one or more perceived defects or flaws in appearance that are not observable or appear only slight to others.
2. Repetitive behaviors (e.g., mirror checking, excessive grooming, skin picking, reassurance seeking) or mental acts (e.g., comparing appearance with others) in response to the appearance concerns.
3. The preoccupation causes clinically significant distress or impairment in social, occupational, or other important areas of functioning.
4. The preoccupation is not better explained by concerns with body fat or weight (as in anorexia nervosa) or muscle size (as in muscle dysmorphia).

To be diagnosed with BDD, a person must meet all of the above criteria. In addition, the preoccupation must not be better explained by another mental health condition. For example, a person with an eating disorder may be concerned with their weight, but this would not be classified as BDD.

Negative Emotions and BDD

People with BDD often experience negative emotions such as shame, embarrassment, anxiety, and depression. These emotions can be triggered by real or perceived flaws in appearance. For example, a person with BDD may feel ashamed of their skin imperfections and avoid social situations for fear of being stared at or ridiculed.

The most typical issues that people with this illness are concerned about include: Excess or misshapen skin, such as wrinkles, scars, acne, and blemishes. Hair of any kind or baldness. Facial features, particularly the nose and the stomach or chest can also be painful.
Other issues include the following: muscles, breasts, thighs, buttock or penis size.

Muscle Dysmorphia

Muscle dysmorphia is a subtype of BDD that is characterized by a preoccupation with the belief that one's body is too small or not muscular enough. People with muscle dysmorphia may spend a lot of time working out, lifting weights, and taking supplements in an attempt to increase their muscle size. Muscle dysmorphia can cause significant distress and impairment in social, occupational, or other important areas of functioning.

The following are some of the core clinical features of muscle dysmorphia:
- People with muscle dysmorphia are preoccupied with the belief that their body is too small or not muscular enough. They may spend a lot of time thinking about their muscles and may compare themselves with others.
- People with muscle dysmorphia may engage in repetitive behaviors such as excessive exercising, lifting weights, and taking supplements. These

behaviors are often an attempt to relieve the anxiety and distress caused by the person's beliefs about their muscles.

- People with muscle dysmorphia may miss work or school, avoid social situations, and have difficulty maintaining relationships.

Body Dysmorphic Disorder by Proxy

Body dysmorphic disorder by proxy (BDD-by-proxy) is a subtype of BDD in which the person is preoccupied with the appearance of someone else. People with BDD-by-proxy may be excessively concerned about minor or nonexistent flaws in the appearance of their child, partner, or another loved one. They may also engage in repetitive and excessive behaviors such as checking, touching, or measuring the person's appearance. BDD-by-proxy can cause significant distress and impairment in social, occupational, or other important areas of functioning.

Delusions in Body Dysmorphic Disorder

Some people with BDD may experience delusions, which are false beliefs that are not based in reality. People with BDD may believe that their appearance defects are real and severe, even when others cannot see them. They may also believe that they are ugly or disgusting, even when they are not. Delusions can cause significant distress and impairment in social, occupational, or other important areas of functioning.

BDD with delusions are completely convinced that they are disfigured somehow and that others take notice and are disgusted by their appearance. They often avoid all social situations for fear of being ridiculed or stared at. People with BDD may also engage in repetitive behaviors such as checking, touching, or measuring their appearance. These behaviors are often an attempt to relieve the anxiety and distress caused by the person's beliefs about their appearance.

Chapter 3: Why Does It Happen?

It's not clear what causes body dysmorphic disorder (BDD). It may be caused by a combination of genetic and environmental factors.

Some people with BDD have a close relative with the condition, which suggests that it may run in families. However, it's not known whether this is due to genetics or a shared environment (such as upbringing).

It's thought that BDD may be associated with problems in the way the brain processes information about body image. People with BDD often have a distorted view of how they look and spend a lot of time worrying about their appearance.

Environmental Factors

As discussed previously, the disease is more prevalent among adolescents. It is believed that the increased use of social media among teens has contributed to the development of BDD.

When people are exposed to images of "perfect" bodies, they may compare themselves to these unrealistic standards and feel inadequate. This can lead to low self-esteem and body image issues.

It's also thought that certain life experiences may trigger BDD or make it worse. For example, being teased about your appearance during childhood or adolescence may increase your risk of developing the condition.
It's also thought that people with BDD may have differences in the way their brains process information about body image. People with BDD have a distorted view of how they look and spend a lot of time worrying about their appearance.

Biological Factors

There is evidence to suggest that certain biological factors may play a role in the development of BDD. For example, people with the condition often have an imbalance of serotonin, a neurotransmitter that helps regulate mood.

Psychological Factors

BDD may also be linked to certain personality traits, such as perfectionism and obsessive-compulsive tendencies. Having BDD can be a way of coping with underlying psychological issues, such as low self-esteem or anxiety.

It's important to remember that BDD is a real mental health condition that can cause significant distress and interfere with your life.

Pathophysiology

The pathophysiology of BDD likely involves a complex interplay of dysfunctions in several brain networks, including those involved in visual processing, emotion, and cognition.

It is thought that people with BDD have abnormalities in the way they process visual information. For example, they may over-value certain aspects of their appearance and dwell on their perceived flaws.

Genetics

Heritability studies suggest that BDD has a strong genetic component. Eight percent of first-degree relatives of people with BDD meet criteria for the disorder, and first-degree relatives are six times more likely to have BDD than the general population.

Twin studies have further shown that genes play a role in the development of BDD. Identical twins are more likely to both have BDD than fraternal twins, and monozygotic twins are more likely to share BDD symptoms than dizygotic twins.

These studies suggest that genetic factors play a role in the development of BDD, although the specific genes involved have yet to be identified.

Recent neuroimaging studies have begun to shed light on the neural basis of BDD. These studies suggest that people with BDD may have abnormalities in the way certain brain regions process visual information.

For example, one study found that people with BDD had increased activity in the right inferior frontal gyrus (rIFG) and right fusiform gyrus (rFFG) when viewing images of their own face. The rIFG is thought to be involved in self-referential processing, and the rFFG is thought to be involved in facial recognition.

Another study found that people with BDD had increased activity in the amygdala, a brain region involved in fear and anxiety, when viewing images of their own face. This suggests that people with BDD may have a heightened fear response when thinking about or seeing their own appearance.

Body Dysmorphia and Temporal Lobe Damage

There is also some evidence to suggest that people with BDD may have damage to the temporal lobes, which are brain regions involved in processing visual information.

One study found that people with BDD were more likely to have had a past head injury than people without BDD. The study also found that people with BDD were more likely to report experiencing a seizure before the age of 15.

Another study found that people with BDD were more likely to have abnormalities in the structure of their temporal lobes. These abnormalities were most pronounced in the right temporal lobe, which is thought to be involved in processing visual information.

Neurochemistry of Body Dysmorphia

Serotonin is a neurotransmitter that helps regulate mood. People with BDD often have an imbalance of serotonin, which may play a role in the development of the condition.

For example, one study found that people with BDD had lower levels of the serotonin metabolite 5-HIAA in their cerebrospinal fluid. This suggests that people with BDD may have reduced serotonin activity in the brain.

Other studies have found that people with BDD are more likely to respond positively to treatment with serotonin-based medications, such as selective serotonin reuptake inhibitors (SSRIs). This further supports the role of serotonin in the development of BDD.

Cognitive Factors

People with BDD often have distorted beliefs about their appearance. For example, they may believe that they are ugly or deformed, even if there is nothing visibly wrong with them.

They may also compare themselves to other people and think that they do not measure up. People with BDD often focus on a specific body part, such as their skin, hair, or nose.

These distorted beliefs may play a role in the development and maintenance of BDD. For example, people with BDD may avoid social situations because they are afraid that other people will notice their flaws and judge them.

They may also engage in compulsive behaviors, such as excessive grooming or mirror checking, in an attempt to improve their appearance. However, these behaviors often make the person with BDD feel more anxious and depressed, which can perpetuate the cycle of BDD.

Risk Factors

There are several risk factors for BDD, including:

- **Family history**. People with a family member who has BDD or another mental health condition are more likely to develop BDD themselves.
- **Age**. BDD is most common in adolescence and young adulthood.
- Gender. BDD is more common in females than in males.
- **Low self-esteem**. People with low self-esteem are more likely to develop BDD.
- **Perfectionism**. People who are perfectionists are more likely to develop BDD.
- **History of abuse or trauma**. People who have experienced abuse or trauma are more likely to develop BDD.

More research is needed to understand the causes of BDD. However, it is likely that a combination of aforementioned genetic, neurobiological, and psychological factors play a role in the development of the condition.

Chapter 4: Who Is Effected?

Body dysmorphia is not limited to any one group of people. It can affect anybody, regardless of age, gender, or background. However, there are some groups who seem to be more susceptible to developing body dysmorphia . In this chapter, we will take a look at some of the most common groups affected by this disorder.

The epidemiology of BDD is not well understood. The disorder is thought to be rare, with a prevalence of 0.7% in the general population. However, the prevalence may be higher in certain populations, such as people with psychiatric disorders and people seeking cosmetic surgery. BDD is more common in women than in men, and the average age of onset is late adolescence or early adulthood.

Body Dysmorphia in Females

Women are more likely than men to develop body dysmorphia. This is likely due to the pressure that society puts on women to look a certain way. There are endless images in the media of what a "perfect" woman looks like, and these ideals can be impossible to live up to.

Not Feminine Enough

One of the most common manifestations of body dysmorphia in women is the belief that they are not feminine enough. This can manifest itself in a number of different ways. For example, a woman may believe that she is too muscular and therefore not feminine enough. She may also believe that she is not pretty enough or that her features are not feminine enough. She may think she is too hairy or that her breasts are too small

This type of body dysmorphia can be extremely distressing for sufferers. They may feel like they are not good enough and that they will never be able to meet society's standards of beauty. This can lead to a downward spiral of negative thoughts and behaviors.

Too Feminine

Another manifestation of body dysmorphia in women is the belief that they are too feminine. This can be due to a number of different factors. For example, a woman may believe that she is too curvy and therefore not attractive. She may also believe that her breasts are too large or that her hips are too wide.

This type of body dysmorphia can be just as distressing as the belief that you are not feminine enough. Women may feel like they are unattractive and that they will never be able to meet society's standards of beauty. This can lead to a downward spiral of negative thoughts and behaviors.

One study found that nearly half of all women surveyed were unhappy with their bodies, and almost a quarter of them felt that they needed to lose weight. This pressure to be thin can lead to unhealthy behaviors, such as crash dieting and excessive exercise. It can also lead to more serious disorders, such as anorexia nervosa and bulimia nervosa.

Big Nose

One of the most common complaints among people with body dysmorphia is that they believe their noses are too big. This can be a very distressing belief, as it can affect a person's self-esteem and confidence. It can also lead to avoidant behaviors, such as not wanting to leave the house or not wanting to talk to people.

A study of college students found that those with body dysmorphic disorder were more likely to have a negative view of their noses. They were also more likely to avoid social situations and to suffer from depression and anxiety.

Acne

Although it can occur in both males and females, acne is a very common complaint among people with body dysmorphia. This is likely due to the fact that acne can be very visible and can affect a person's self-esteem.

A study of adolescents found that those with body dysmorphic disorder were more likely to have a negative view of their skin.

Body Dysmorphia in Males

Although body dysmorphia is more common in women, it can still affect men. In fact, the number of men affected by body dysmorphia is on the rise. This is likely due to the pressure that society puts on men to look a certain way. There are endless images in the media of what a "perfect" man looks like, and these ideals can be impossible to live up to.

Not Masculine Enough

One of the most common manifestations of body dysmorphia in men is the belief that they are not masculine enough. This can manifest itself in a number of different ways. For example, a man may believe that he is too skinny and therefore not masculine enough. He may also believe that he is not tall enough or that his features are not masculine enough.

This type of body dysmorphia can be extremely distressing for sufferers. They may feel like they are not good enough and that they will never be able to meet society's standards of beauty. This can lead to a downward spiral of negative thoughts and behaviors.

Baldness

Another common manifestation of body dysmorphia in men is the belief that they are balding. This can be a very distressing belief, as it can lead to feelings of insecurity and inadequacy. Men may feel like they are not attractive and that they will never be able to meet society's standards of beauty. This can lead to a downward spiral of negative thoughts and behaviors.

Body Dysmorphic Disorder in Children

Although it is a condition that most often occurs in adults, its onset can be traced back to adolescence and sometimes even childhood. Children with Body Dysmorphic Disorder (BDD) tend to fixate on a specific body part or aspect of their appearance that they find unacceptable. The preoccupation is so intense that it causes significant distress and impairment in functioning. In children, the condition often co-occurs with anxiety disorders such as social anxiety disorder, separation anxiety disorder, and specific phobias.

Different than Normal Worrying

Most children go through phases where they are self-conscious or dissatisfied with their appearance. For example, a child may worry that they are too skinny or that they have a "big nose." However, these worries are usually temporary and do not cause significant distress or impairment in functioning.

In contrast, children with BDD obsess over their perceived flaws to the point where it causes significant distress and impairment in functioning. For example, a child with BDD may miss school because they are too afraid to leave the house or they may refuse to go to parties or sleepovers because they are embarrassed about their appearance.

Body Dysmorphia Across Cultures and Ethnicities

There is a common misconception that body dysmorphia is a disorder that only affects white, middle-class women. However, this is not the case. Body dysmorphia can affect people of all cultures and ethnicities.

A study of Chinese adolescents found that those with body dysmorphic disorder were more likely to have a negative view of their skin. These studies suggest that body dysmorphic disorder is a culturally diverse disorder that can affect people of all cultures and ethnicities.

Chapter 5: Body Dysmorphia and Comorbidities

Body Dysmorphia in itself is a debilitating disorder. It's not just the physical appearance that people with body dysmorphia are obsessively worried about. Often, they will also have comorbid conditions that can deeply affect their quality of life. These might include depression, anxiety, eating disorders, and substance abuse.

Psychological Comorbidities

Obsessive Compulsive Disorder (OCD) is often comorbid with Body Dysmorphic Disorder. In fact, about 1 in 3 people with BDD also have OCD. This makes sense, as both disorders are characterized by obsessive, intrusive thoughts. For people with BDD, these thoughts focus on perceived flaws in their appearance. For people with OCD, the thoughts can be about anything, and are often accompanied by compulsions, or repetitive behaviors meant to alleviate the anxiety caused by the obsessions.

Depression is common in people with body dysmorphia. This is not surprising, given that people with body dysmorphia are constantly thinking about their flaws and how they are inadequate. They might also be isolating themselves from friends and family, which can lead to feelings of loneliness and isolation. Depression can make it hard to function in everyday life and can even lead to suicidal thoughts. Suicide risk is high in people with BDD, with about 1 in 4 people with the disorder attempting suicide at some point in their lives.

Anxiety is also common in people with body dysmorphia. This is because they are constantly worrying about their appearance and whether or not people are judging them. They might avoid going out in public or even leave the house. This can lead to social isolation and feelings of anxiety.

Eating disorders are often comorbid with body dysmorphia. This is because people with body dysmorphia often have a distorted view of their bodies and think that they are larger than they actually are. As a result, they might start restricting their food intake or purging after eating. Eating disorders can lead to serious health problems, such as malnutrition, organ damage, and even death.

Substance abuse is another common comorbidity of body dysmorphia. People with body dysmorphia might turn to drugs or alcohol to cope with their anxiety and depression. They might also use substances to change their appearance, such as steroids to build muscle or diet pills to lose weight. Substance abuse can lead to addiction and other serious health problems.

Avoidant personality disorder is a disorder that is often comorbid with body dysmorphia. People with this disorder have a fear of rejection and are very sensitive to criticism. As a result, they might avoid social situations or activities that they think might lead to them being judged. This can severely impact their quality of life.

Associated Personality Traits

There are certain personality traits that are often associated with body dysmorphia. People with body dysmorphia might be perfectionists or have high standards for themselves. They might also be very self-critical and have low self-esteem. Often, people with body dysmorphia will compare themselves to others and feel that they fall short. These personality traits can make it difficult for people with body dysmorphia to function in everyday life.

Low self-esteem and neuroticism are significantly associated with body dysmorphic disorder. People with BDD have a negative self-image and see themselves as ugly or deformed. They are also more likely to be anxious, depressed and paranoid.

Unassertiveness, social anxiety and shyness are also associated with BDD. People with BDD might avoid social situations or activities because they are afraid of being judged. They might also have difficulty speaking up for themselves or assertiveness.
Rejection sensitivity and perfectionism are also associated with body dysmorphic disorder. People with BDD tend to be sensitive to rejection and might avoid social situations or activities because they are afraid of being rejected. They might also have high standards for themselves and feel that they need to be perfect in order to be accepted.

Self-criticism is another personality trait that is often associated with body dysmorphia. People with body dysmorphia are constantly critiquing their appearance and thinking that they are not good enough. They might also have a negative view of themselves and think that they are ugly or deformed.

Cognitive Distortions

There are certain cognitive distortions that are often associated with body dysmorphia. People with body dysmorphia might have a distorted view of their bodies and think that they are larger than they actually are. They might also focus on one or two aspects of their appearance and magnify them to the point where they become obsessed. As a result, people with body dysmorphia often have a negative self-image and see themselves as ugly or deformed.

Other cognitive distortions that are often associated with body dysmorphia include all-or-nothing thinking, black-and-white thinking, and overgeneralization. People with body dysmorphia might see themselves as either perfect or imperfect. They might also think that if they are not perfect, then they are worthless. As a result, people with body dysmorphia often have difficulty accepting themselves for who they are.

Physical Comorbidities

People with body dysmorphia often have physical comorbidities as well. This is because the constant worry and stress can take a toll on the body. Some of the common physical comorbidities include headaches, gastrointestinal problems, and sleep disorders.

Headaches are common in people with body dysmorphia. This is because the constant stress and worry can lead to muscle tension and headaches. Gastrointestinal problems are also common, as the constant stress can lead to stomach pain, diarrhea, and constipation. Sleep disorders are also common in people with body dysmorphia. This is because the anxiety and stress can make it hard to fall asleep and stay asleep.

Obsessive Rituals and BDD

People with body dysmorphia often engage in obsessive rituals in an attempt to fix their perceived flaws. These rituals can include excessive grooming, skin picking, and mirror checking. People with body dysmorphia might also avoid mirrors altogether or wear clothes that cover their bodies.

Excessive grooming is one of the most common obsessive rituals in people with body dysmorphia. This can include excessive hair removal, skin care, and makeup. People with body dysmorphia might also pick at their skin in an attempt to fix perceived imperfections. Mirror checking is another common obsessive ritual. People with body dysmorphic disorder often check mirrors frequently to see if their appearance has changed. They might also avoid mirrors altogether because they are afraid of what they might see.

Wearing clothes that cover the body is another common way that people with body dysmorphia try to hide their perceived flaws. They might wear baggy clothes or layers of clothing to cover up their bodies. People with body dysmorphia might also avoid certain activities or situations where their bodies might be exposed.

Chapter 6: Recommended Treatments

Body dysmorphic disorder (BDD) is a challenging condition to assess and treat. Individuals with BDD can be difficult to engage in treatment, due to the nature of their illness. They may be very resistant to discussing their appearance or may avoid people altogether. They may also be fixated on seeking treatments that will never improve their appearance to their satisfaction.

In addition, individuals with BDD often seek multiple cosmetic treatments and surgeries, which can be expensive and may not improve their appearance or self-esteem. As a result, clinicians must be very careful in how they approach treatment for BDD.

The first step in treating BDD is to conduct a thorough assessment. This assessment should include a discussion of the individual's concerns about their appearance, as well as a review of their medical history and any previous treatments they have tried. It is also important to assess for comorbid conditions, such as depression, anxiety, eating disorders, and substance abuse.

Cognitive Behavioral Therapy

Once the assessment is complete, the clinician can work with the individual to develop a treatment plan. The most effective treatment for BDD is cognitive-behavioral therapy (CBT).

CBT promotes the adoption of dysfunctional appearance-related beliefs and exposure to feared and avoided situations by identifying them and logically debating them, as well as response prevention for feared and avoided events. It works by educating the patient on mental and emotional processes that perpetuate their BDD, and then helping them to correct these thought patterns.

CBT has been shown to be effective in reducing symptoms of BDD, and it is the only treatment with evidence-based support.

Exposure Response Prevention

One specific type of CBT that has been shown to be effective in treating BDD is exposure response prevention (ERP). ERP involves gradually exposing the patient to their feared situations and thoughts while teaching them how to prevent themselves from engaging in compulsive behaviors.
For example, a patient with BDD who is afraid of going outside may be asked to spend increasing amounts of time outside, starting with just a few minutes. The patient would then be taught how to prevent themselves from engaging in compulsive behaviors, such as Checking the mirror excessively or picking at their skin.

ERP has been shown to be an effective treatment for BDD, with studies showing that it can lead to improvements in BDD symptoms, quality of life, and functioning.

CBT can be delivered in individual or group therapy format, and usually consists of 10-20 weekly sessions. The success of CBT depends on the motivation of the patient to change their thinking and behavior.
Advance cognitive-behavioral techniques, such as schema focused therapy and dialectical behavior therapy, may be necessary for patients who do not respond to traditional CBT. They are used to address the negative thinking patterns and emotional regulation difficulties that can fuel BDD.

Motivational Interviewing

Motivational interviewing is a technique that can be used to engage individuals in treatment who are resistant or ambivalent about change.

The therapist works with the patient to explore their motivation for change and to identify any ambivalence about making changes in their appearance-related beliefs or behaviors.

Motivational interviewing has been shown to be an effective technique for engaging individuals with BDD in treatment in patients that lack insight.

Pharmacotherapy and Other Somatic Treatments

In addition to CBT, medication may be prescribed to help treat symptoms of BDD. Selective serotonin reuptake inhibitors (SSRIs) are the most commonly prescribed type of medication for BDD.

Other types of medications that have been used to treat BDD include tricyclic antidepressants, antipsychotics, and mood stabilizers.

These medications can be helpful in reducing anxiety and improving mood, but they do not address the underlying thoughts and beliefs that cause BDD. As a result, they are often used in conjunction with CBT.

In some cases, other types of somatic treatments may be recommended. These can include botulinum toxin injections, dermabrasion, and laser surgery. These treatments can be effective in improving the appearance of skin blemishes or wrinkles, but they do not address the underlying body dysmorphic thoughts and beliefs. As a result, they are often used in conjunction with CBT.

The decision to pursue any type of treatment for BDD should be made in consultation with a qualified mental health professional.

Individuals with BDD often have a difficult time seeking treatment due to the shame and embarrassment associated with their condition. It is important to remember that BDD is a real and treatable illness, and there is no shame in seeking help. Treatment should be sought from a qualified mental health professional.

Cognitive-behavioral therapy is the most effective treatment for BDD, and it is the only treatment with evidence-based support. Medication may also be prescribed to help treat symptoms of BDD, but it is important to remember that medication does not address the underlying thoughts and beliefs that cause BDD. As a result, CBT should always be used in conjunction with medication.

Treatment of Children and Adolescents with BDD

The treatment of children and adolescents with BDD is similar to the treatment of adults. CBT is the most effective treatment, and it is the only treatment with evidence-based support. Medication may also be prescribed to help treat symptoms of BDD, but it is important to remember that medication does not address the underlying thoughts and beliefs that cause BDD. As a result, CBT should always be used in conjunction with medication.

When treating children and adolescents with BDD, it is important to involve the parents or guardians in the treatment process. Parents or guardians can provide support and guidance to help the child or adolescent make changes in their thinking and behavior. In some cases, it may also be necessary to involve other family members or professionals, such as teachers or counselors.

It is important to remember that BDD is a real and treatable illness. If you or someone you know is struggling with BDD, please seek help from a qualified mental health professional.

Chapter 7: Cosmetic Treatment

Body dysmorphic disorder (BDD) is a severe mental disorder characterized by a preoccupation with an imagined or slight defect in appearance. People with BDD may undergo cosmetic treatments, including surgery, to try to "fix" their appearance. Unfortunately, these procedures rarely relieve the distress caused by BDD and may even make the problem worse.

After cognitive therapy, people with BDD may still want to pursue cosmetic treatments. In these cases, it is important to work with a mental health professional and/or dermatologist who understands BDD to make sure that any procedures are done in a way that minimizes the risk of making the problem worse.

It is also important to be aware that people with BDD often seek out multiple cosmetic treatments, sometimes from different practitioners. This can lead to a cycle of dissatisfaction, as the person is never quite satisfied with the results.

Surgical Treatments

People with BDD may seek out various types of surgery to "fix" their appearance. Unfortunately, surgery rarely alleviates the distress caused by BDD and may even make the problem worse.

The most common surgical procedures sought by people with BDD include: rhinoplasty (nose surgery), otoplasty (ear surgery), blepharoplasty (eyelid surgery), facelift, breast augmentation or reduction, and liposuction.

Rhinoplasty is the most commonly requested surgical procedure among people with BDD. Unfortunately, it is also one of the least likely to result in satisfaction. In a study of 100 people with BDD who underwent rhinoplasty, only 5% reported being "very satisfied" with the results and 25% were actually dissatisfied with the outcome.

Otoplasty, or ear surgery, is another common procedure requested by people with BDD. As with rhinoplasty, satisfaction rates are low, with only about 15% of patients reporting being "very satisfied" with the results.

Blepharoplasty, or eyelid surgery, is another common surgical procedure sought by people with BDD. In a study of 100 people with BDD who underwent blepharoplasty, only 14% reported being "very satisfied" with the results.

Facelift is another surgical procedure that is sometimes sought by people with BDD. In a study of 100 people with BDD who underwent facelift, only 11% reported being "very satisfied" with the results.

Breast augmentation or reduction is sometimes requested by women with BDD. In a study of 100 women with BDD who underwent breast surgery, only 9% reported being "very satisfied" with the results.

Liposuction is sometimes requested by people with BDD, particularly those who are concerned about their weight or body shape. In a study of 100 people with BDD who underwent liposuction, only 8% reported being "very satisfied" with the results.

Dermatologic Treatments

In addition to surgical procedures, people with BDD may also seek out various types of dermatologic and cosmetic treatments. These include: hair transplants, Botox injections, dermabrasion, laser skin resurfacing, and fillers (such as collagen or fat injections).

As with surgical procedures, the satisfaction rates for these types of treatments are generally low. In a study of 100 people with BDD who underwent hair transplants, only 5% reported being "very satisfied" with the results.

Injections of botulinum toxin (Botox) are sometimes used to treat wrinkles or other perceived imperfections.

Dermabrasion is a procedure that uses a rotating brush to remove the top layer of skin. It is sometimes used to improve the appearance of scars or other blemishes. Laser skin resurfacing is a procedure that uses a laser to remove the top layer of skin. It is sometimes used to improve the appearance of wrinkles, scars, or other blemishes.

Fillers are substances that are injected into the skin to fill in wrinkles or other perceived imperfections. They can be made from various materials, such as collagen, fat, or silicone.

Evaluation of BDD Patients Seeking Cosmetic Treatment

It is important to note that people with BDD are often dissatisfied with the results of cosmetic procedures, regardless of the outcome. This dissatisfaction can lead to a number of negative consequences, including:

- Continued anxiety and distress about their appearance
- Further efforts to "fix" their appearance, often leading to more surgery or other procedures
- Increased use of substances (e.g., alcohol, drugs) to cope with distress
- Social isolation
- Suicide

Because of these risks, it is important for anyone considering cosmetic treatment to be evaluated by a mental health professional first. This evaluation should include a thorough assessment of the person's BDD symptoms, as well as their psychological history and current mental state. Only after such an evaluation should a decision be made about whether or not to proceed with treatment.

Risks Assessment

As with any type of surgery or medical procedure, there are risks associated with cosmetic treatments. These risks include: Anesthesia-related risks, bleeding, infection, nerve damage, scarring and allergic reactions.

It is important to discuss these risks with a qualified medical professional before undergoing any type of cosmetic procedure.

Treatment of Comorbid Conditions

People with BDD often suffer from other psychiatric conditions as well, such as depression, anxiety disorders, and eating disorders. These comorbid conditions can make the symptoms of BDD worse and make treatment more difficult. Therefore, it is important to treat any comorbid conditions along with BDD.

Psychotherapy

Psychotherapy is the most common form of treatment for BDD. It can be conducted individually, in a group setting, or with family members. The goals of psychotherapy are to:

- Reduce distress and improve functioning
- Help the person develop a more realistic view of their appearance
- Teach coping and problem-solving skills
- Address any comorbid conditions

Remember, Body Dysmorphia is a treatable mental illness with a number of effective treatment options.

Chapter 8: Family Members and Friends as Agents of Change

Body Dysmorphia is often reported by a family member or a friend, instead of the patient themselves. This can be for a variety of reasons. The person with Body Dysmorphia may not be able to see their own dysmorphia, they may be too embarrassed to talk about it, or they may not realize that what they are experiencing is abnormal.

Whether you are reading this as a parent, sibling, friend, or other loved one of someone with BDD, know that you can make a difference. The right kind of support and encouragement from family and friends is crucial for someone with BDD. In fact, research has shown that social support is associated with better mental health outcomes, including for those with BDD.

At the same time, it's important to understand that you cannot "fix" BDD or make it go away. It is a real and serious mental health condition that requires professional treatment. But as a loved one, you can play an important role in supporting your loved one's treatment and recovery.

What To Do

Here are some things you can do to help:

Educate Yourself

Learn about BDD. The more you know about BDD, the better equipped you will be to support your loved one. Read books and articles, talk to other families, and attend conferences or support groups (if available in your area).

The International OCD Foundation (IOCDF) is a great resource for learning about BDD and finding treatment providers. You can also check out the resources section of this website for more information.

Be There, Listen and Believe

Make yourself available to your loved one. Show that you care and want to help. Let them know that you are there for them, no matter what. Listen to your loved one without judgment. Avoid giving advice or trying to "fix" them. Just let them know that you hear them and that you believe them.

Validate Their Feelings

Acknowledge that BDD is a real and serious mental health condition. It is not their fault and they are not making it up. Reassure them that you understand how difficult it is to live with BDD.

Encourage Treatment

BDD is a treatable condition, but treatment requires professional help. Encourage your loved one to seek treatment from a mental health professional with experience treating BDD. You can also offer to go with them to their appointments or help them find a treatment provider.

Offer Practical Support

There are many ways you can offer practical support to someone with BDD. You can help them with day-to-day tasks, such as shopping or driving. You can also offer to go with them to doctor's appointments or other treatment appointments.

You might also consider helping them create a "bail-out plan" for times when their BDD is particularly bad. This can include things like having a list of distractions or activities to do when they are feeling triggered, or having someone they can call for support in moments of need.

Be Patient

Recovery from BDD takes time. It is important to be patient and encourage your loved one to stick with treatment, even when it is difficult. Remember that there will be good days and bad days.

What Not To Do

There are also some things you should avoid doing, as they can make the situation worse. Here are some things to avoid:

Don't Enable Their BDD

BDD can be a very debilitating condition, but it is important not to enable your loved one's BDD by accommodating their compulsions or avoidance behaviors. For example, don't agree to drive them places they would normally avoid because of their fear of being seen in public. Instead, encourage them to face their fears and get out of the house.

Don't Participate in Their Compulsions

Avoid participating in your loved one's compulsions or rituals. This includes things like reassuring them or agreeing to look at their flaws with them. This will only reinforce their BDD and make it harder for them to recover.

Don't Criticize Their Appearance

It is important not to criticize your loved one's appearance, as this can make their BDD worse. Instead, focus on their inner qualities and strengths.

Don't Take Their BDD Personally

BDD is not about you. It is important not to take your loved one's BDD personally. Their BDD is not a reflection of how they feel about you or your relationship.

Seek Professional Help

If you are struggling to cope with your own emotions or you are finding it difficult to support your loved one, seek professional help. There are many therapists and counselors who specialize in supporting families dealing with mental health conditions.

Parting Words

Wanting to look perfect is an understandable and common desire. However, for some people, this desire becomes all-consuming and takes over their lives. When this reflection and preoccupation takes over your life to the point where it interferes with daily functioning, it may be indicative of a condition known as body dysmorphic disorder (BDD).

It is about the ideal body aesthetic that is being projected to the world, and it affects both men and women of all ages. It usually starts during adolescence but can also develop in childhood or adulthood.

Please remember that it is not just a phase, and it is a real mental health condition that requires professional treatment. With proper diagnosis and treatment, people with BDD can learn to manage their symptoms and live fulfilling lives.

If you or someone you know is struggling with BDD, please seek professional help. The earlier the diagnosis and treatment, the better the prognosis. There is no shame in seeking help , and we hope that this book has been a helpful resource for you.